JOINING WITH DC

When instructed to join with dc, begin with a slip knot on hook. YO, holding loop on hook, insert hook in stitch or space indicated, YO and pull up a loop (3 loops on hook), (YO and draw through 2 loops on hook) twice.

FREE LOOPS OF A CHAIN

When instructed to work in free loops of a chain, work in loop indicated by arrow *(Fig. 1)*.

Fig. 1

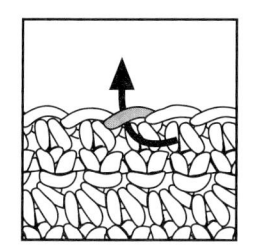

BACK OR FRONT LOOP ONLY

Work only in loop(s) indicated by arrow *(Fig. 2)*.

Fig. 2

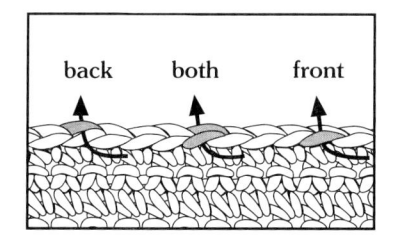

WORKING IN SPACE BEFORE A STITCH

When instructed to work in space before a stitch or in spaces between stitches, insert hook in space indicated by arrow *(Fig. 3)*.

Fig. 3

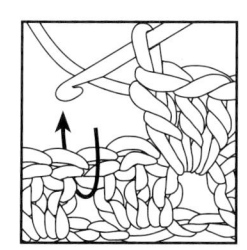

LOOP STITCH

Insert hook in stitch, wrap yarn around finger, insert hook through loops on finger *(Fig. 4a & Fig. 4b)*, draw through st, remove finger from loops, YO and draw through all 3 loops on hook pulling each loop to measure approximately 1¹/₂" *(Loop St made, Fig. 4c)*.

Fig. 4a Fig. 4b 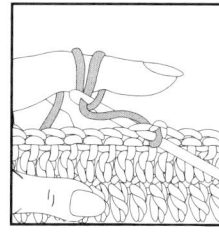 Fig. 4c

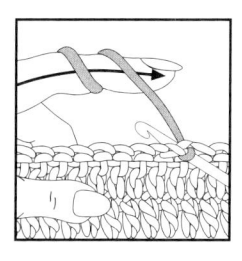

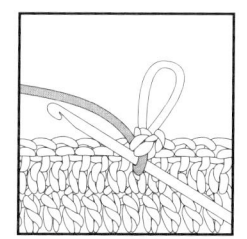

WHIPSTITCH

Place two Squares or pieces with **wrong** sides together. Sew through both pieces once to secure the beginning of the seam, leaving an ample yarn end to weave in later. Insert the needle from **front** to **back** through **both** loops on **both** pieces *(Fig. 5a)* **or** through **inside** loops only of each stitch on **both** pieces *(Fig. 5b)*. Bring the needle around and insert it from **front** to **back** through next loops of both pieces. Continue in this manner across, keeping the sewing yarn fairly loose.

Fig. 5a Fig. 5b

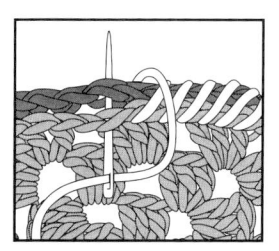

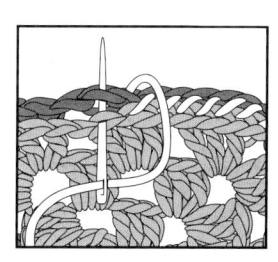

SIZE NOTE

Instructions are written for size Small, with sizes Medium and Large in braces { }. Instructions will be easier to read if you circle all the numbers pertaining to your size. If only one number is given it applies to all sizes. *(See handy ruler on inside back cover.)*

NO SLIP FINISHING

To provide traction on bottom Sole of each Slipper, use dimensional fabric paint to add rows of wavy lines or dots as desired to heel and toe; let paint dry completely.

1. FUZZY WUZZIES

Shown on Front Cover. **EASY**
Designed by Modene Thornton

See Size Note, page 2.

WOMEN'S SLIPPERS

Small	Medium	Large
9" (23 cm)	9^1/$_2$" (24 cm)	10" (25.5 cm)

MATERIALS
Worsted Weight Yarn: **MEDIUM 4**
  6^1/$_2$ {6^3/$_4$-7} ounces
  360{370-385} yards
  180{190-200} grams
  329{338.5-352} meters
Crochet hook as indicated below **or** size needed for gauge
  Size Small: size G (4 mm)
  Size Medium: size H (5 mm)
  Size Large: size I (5.5 mm)
Yarn needle
Stiff bristled brush

GAUGE: 16{14-12} sc and 16{14-12} rows = 4" (10 cm)

Gauge Swatch: 4" (10 cm)
Ch 17{15-13}.
Row 1: Sc in second ch from hook and in each ch across: 16{14-12} sc.
Rows 2 thru 16{14-12}: Ch 1, turn; sc in each sc across.
Finish off.

SLIPPER
SOLE
Ch 26.

Rnd 1 (Right side)**:** 2 Sc in second ch from hook, sc in next 10 chs, hdc in next 3 chs, dc in next 8 chs, 2 dc in next ch, hdc in next ch, 5 sc in last ch (toe); working in free loops of beginning ch *(Fig. 1, page 2)*, hdc in next ch, 2 dc in next ch, dc in next 8 chs, hdc in next 3 chs, sc in next 10 chs, 2 sc in same ch as first sc; do **not** join, place marker *(see Markers, page 1)*: 57 sts.

Note: Loop a short piece of yarn around any stitch to mark Rnd 1 as **right** side.

Rnd 2: 2 Sc in each of next 2 sc, sc in next 24 sts, 2 sc in next sc, (sc in next sc, 2 sc in next sc) twice, sc in next 24 sts, 2 sc in each of next 2 sc: 64 sc.

Rnd 3: Sc in next sc, 2 sc in next sc, sc in next 25 sc, 2 sc in next sc, (sc in next 2 sc, 2 sc in next sc) 3 times, sc in next 25 sc, 2 sc in next sc, sc in next sc: 70 sc.

Rnd 4: Sc in next sc, 2 sc in next sc, sc in next 28 sc, 2 sc in next sc, (sc in next 2 sc, 2 sc in next sc) 3 times, sc in next 28 sc, 2 sc in next sc, sc in next sc: 76 sc.

Rnd 5: Sc in next 35 sc, 2 sc in next sc, sc in next 4 sc, 2 sc in next sc, sc in next 35 sc; do **not** finish off: 78 sc.

SIDES

Rnd 1 (Wrong side)**:** Ch 1, turn; work Loop Stitch in each sc around *(Figs. 4a-c, page 2)*: 78 Loop Sts.

Rnds 2-10: Work Loop Stitch in each Loop Stitch around.

Rnd 11: Slip st tightly in each Loop Stitch around; finish off.

INSTEP SEAM

With **right** sides together, flatten Slipper lengthwise, matching slip sts on Rnd 11 of Sides; working through **both** loops and beginning at toe, whipstitch a 4" (10 cm) seam *(Fig. 5a, page 2)*, leave remaining slip sts unsewn for opening.
Cut all loops and brush to resemble fur.

CHILDREN'S SLIPPERS

Small	Medium	Large
7 1/2" (19 cm)	8" (20.5 cm)	8 1/2" (21.5 cm)

MATERIALS

Worsted Weight Yarn: **MEDIUM 4**
  5 1/4{5 3/4-6} ounces
  290{315-330} yards
  150{160-170} grams
  265{288-302} meters
Crochet hook as indicated below **or** size needed for gauge
  Size Small: size G (4 mm)
  Size Medium: size H (5 mm)
  Size Large: size I (5.5 mm)
Yarn needle
Stiff bristled brush

GAUGE: 16{14-12} sc and 16{14-12} rows = 4" (10 cm)

Gauge Swatch: 4" (10 cm)
Ch 17{15-13}.
Row 1: Sc in second ch from hook and in each ch across: 16{14-12} sc.
Rows 2 thru 16{14-12}: Ch 1, turn; sc in each sc across.
Finish off.

SLIPPER
SOLE
Ch 22.

Rnd 1 (Right side)**:** 2 Sc in second ch from hook, sc in next 8 chs, hdc in next 3 chs, dc in next 6 chs, 2 dc in next ch, hdc in next ch, 5 sc in last ch (toe); working in free loops of beginning ch *(Fig. 1, page 2)*, hdc in next ch, 2 dc in next ch, dc in next 6 chs, hdc in next 3 chs, sc in next 8 chs, 2 sc in same ch as first sc; do **not** join, place marker *(see Markers, page 1)*: 49 sts.

Note: Loop a short piece of yarn around any stitch to mark Rnd 1 as **right** side.

Rnd 2: 2 Sc in each of next 2 sc, sc in next 20 sts, 2 sc in next sc, (sc in next sc, 2 sc in next sc) twice, sc in next 20 sts, 2 sc in each of next 2 sc: 56 sc.

Rnd 3: Sc in next sc, 2 sc in next sc, sc in next 21 sc, 2 sc in next sc, (sc in next 2 sc, 2 sc in next sc) 3 times, sc in next 21 sc, 2 sc in next sc, sc in next sc: 62 sc.

Rnd 4: Sc in next sc, 2 sc in next sc, sc in next 24 sc, 2 sc in next sc, (sc in next 2 sc, 2 sc in next sc) 3 times, sc in next 24 sc, 2 sc in next sc, sc in next sc: 68 sc.

Rnd 5: Sc in next 31 sc, 2 sc in next sc, sc in next 4 sc, 2 sc in next sc, sc in next 31 sc; do **not** finish off: 70 sc.

SIDES

Rnd 1 (Wrong side)**:** Ch 1, turn; work Loop Stitch in each sc around *(Figs. 4a-c, page 2)*: 70 Loop Sts.

Rnds 2-8: Work Loop Stitch in each Loop Stitch around.

Rnd 9: Slip st tightly in each Loop Stitch around; finish off.

INSTEP SEAM

With **right** sides together, flatten Slipper lengthwise, matching slip sts on Rnd 9 of Sides; working through **both** loops and beginning at toe, whipstitch a 4" (10 cm) seam *(Fig. 5a, page 2)*, leave remaining slip sts unsewn for opening.
Cut all loops and brush to resemble fur.

2. LILAC SQUARES

Shown on Back Cover. **EASY**
Designed by Knit 'N' Purl Shop

See Size Note, page 2.

WOMEN'S SLIPPERS

Small	Medium	Large
9" (23 cm)	9$\frac{1}{2}$" (24 cm)	10" (25.5 cm)

MATERIALS
Worsted Weight Yarn: **MEDIUM 4**
- Dk Green - 2$\frac{1}{4}${2$\frac{1}{4}$-2$\frac{1}{2}$} ounces
  125{125-140} yards
  65{65-70} grams
  114.5{114.5-128} meters
- Green - 80{80-120} yards
  73{73-109.5} meters
- Purple - 40{40-60} yards
  36.5{36.5-55} meters
- Crochet hook as indicated below **or** size needed for gauge
  - **Size Small and Medium:** size E (3.5 mm)
  - **Size Large:** size F (3.75 mm)
- Yarn needle

GAUGE: Size Small, Square = 3$\frac{1}{2}$" (9 cm)
Size Medium, Square = 3$\frac{3}{4}$" (9.5 cm)
Size Large, Square = 4$\frac{1}{2}$" (11.5 cm)

Gauge Swatch: Work same as Square.

SLIPPER
SQUARE (Make 6)
With Purple, ch 3, join with slip st to form a ring.

Rnd 1 (Right side): Ch 3 (**counts as first dc, now and throughout**), 2 dc in ring, ch 1, (3 dc in ring, ch 1) 3 times; join with slip st to first dc, finish off: 12 dc and 4 ch-1 sps.

Note: Loop a short piece of yarn around any stitch to mark Rnd 1 as **right** side.

Rnd 2: With **right** side facing, join Green with dc in any ch-1 sp (*see Joining With Dc, page 2*); (2 dc, ch 1, 3 dc) in same sp, (3 dc, ch 1, 3 dc) in next 3 ch-1 sps; join with slip st to first dc, finish off: 24 dc and 4 ch-1 sps.

Rnd 3: With **right** side facing, join Dk Green with dc in any ch-1 sp; (2 dc, ch 1, 3 dc) in same sp, skip next 3 dc, 3 dc in sp **before** next dc (**Fig. 3, page 2**), ★ (3 dc, ch 1, 3 dc) in next ch-1 sp, skip next 3 dc, 3 dc in sp **before** next dc; repeat from ★ 2 times **more**; join with slip st to first dc, do **not** finish off: 36 dc and 4 ch-1 sps.

SIZE SMALL ONLY
Rnd 4: Ch 1, sc in same st and in next 2 dc, 3 sc in next ch-1 sp, (sc in next 9 dc, 3 sc in next ch-1 sp) 3 times, sc in last 6 dc; join with slip st to first sc, finish off: 48 sc.

SIZE MEDIUM ONLY
Rnd 4: Ch 2 (**counts as first hdc**), hdc in next 2 dc, 3 hdc in next ch-1 sp, (hdc in next 9 dc, 3 hdc in next ch-1 sp) 3 times, hdc in last 6 dc; join with slip st to first hdc, finish off: 48 hdc.

SIZE LARGE ONLY
Rnd 4: Slip st in next 2 dc and in next ch-1 sp, ch 3, (2 dc, ch 1, 3 dc) in same sp, (skip next 3 dc, 3 dc in sp **before** next dc) twice, ★ (3 dc, ch 1, 3 dc) in next ch-1 sp, (skip next 3 dc, 3 dc in sp **before** next dc) twice; repeat from ★ 2 times **more**; join with slip st to first dc, finish off: 48 dc and 4 ch-1 sps.

ASSEMBLY
With Dk Green, **wrong** sides together and working through **inside** loops only, whipstitch Squares together (*Fig. 5b, page 2*) forming 2 vertical strips of 2 Squares each; then whipstitch strips together. Form heel by joining Square 5 to corner (*Diagram 1*); then form toe by joining Square 6 to opposite corner and to Square 1 and Square 3 (*Diagram 2*).

Diagram 1

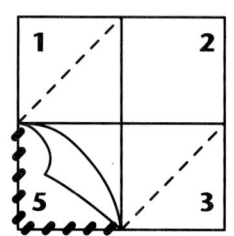

Diagram 2

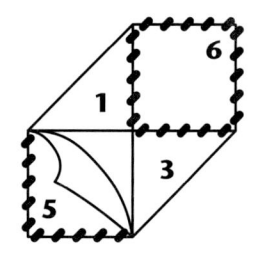

3. PURPLE PASSION

Shown on Back Cover. ■■□□ EASY
Designed by Modene Thornton

See Size Note, page 2.

WOMEN'S SLIPPERS

Small	Medium	Large
9" (23 cm)	9½" (24 cm)	10" (25.5 cm)

MATERIALS
Worsted Weight Yarn: **MEDIUM 4**
- White - 4¾{5-5¼} ounces
  - 265{280-290} yards
  - 135{140-150} grams
  - 242.5{256-265} meters
- Purple - 2¾{3-3¼} ounces
  - 155{170-180} yards
  - 80{90-95} grams
  - 141.5{155.5-164.5} meters

Crochet hook as indicated below **or** size needed for gauge
- **Size Small:** size G (4 mm)
- **Size Medium:** size H (5 mm)
- **Size Large:** size I (5.5 mm)

Stiff bristled brush
Yarn needle

GAUGE: 16{14-12} sc
and 16{14-12} rows = 4" (10 cm)

Gauge Swatch: 4" (10 cm)
With Purple, ch 17{15-13}.
Row 1: Sc in second ch from hook and in each ch across: 16{14-12} sc.
Rows 2 thru 16{14-12}: Ch 1, turn; sc in each sc across.
Finish off.

STITCH GUIDE

SC DECREASE
Pull up a loop in next 2 sc on Sides, YO and draw through all 3 loops on hook **(counts as one sc)**.

BEGINNING DC DECREASE (uses next 2 sc)
Ch 3, ★ YO, insert hook in **next** sc, YO and pull up a loop, YO and draw through 2 loops on hook; repeat from ★ once **more**, YO and draw through all 3 loops on hook **(counts as one dc)**.

DC DECREASE (uses next 3 sc)
★ YO, insert hook in **next** sc, YO and pull up a loop, YO and draw through 2 loops on hook; repeat from ★ 2 times **more**, YO and draw through all 4 loops on hook **(counts as one dc)**.

SLIPPER
SOLE
With Purple, ch 26.

Rnd 1 (Right side): 2 Sc in second ch from hook, sc in next 10 chs, hdc in next 3 chs, dc in next 8 chs, 2 dc in next ch, hdc in next ch, 5 sc in last ch (toe); working in free loops of beginning ch *(Fig. 1, page 2)*, hdc in next ch, 2 dc in next ch, dc in next 8 chs, hdc in next 3 chs, sc in next 10 chs, 2 sc in same ch as first sc; do **not** join; place marker *(see Markers, page 1)*: 57 sts.

Note: Loop a short piece of yarn around any stitch to mark Rnd 1 as **right** side.

Rnd 2: 2 Sc in each of next 2 sc, sc in next 24 sts, 2 sc in next sc, (sc in next sc, 2 sc in next sc) twice, sc in next 24 sts, 2 sc in each of next 2 sc: 64 sc.

Rnd 3: Sc in next sc, 2 sc in next sc, sc in next 25 sc, 2 sc in next sc, (sc in next 2 sc, 2 sc in next sc) 3 times, sc in next 25 sc, 2 sc in next sc, sc in next sc: 70 sc.

Rnd 4: Sc in next sc, 2 sc in next sc, sc in next 28 sc, 2 sc in next sc, (sc in next 2 sc, 2 sc in next sc) 3 times, sc in next 28 sc, 2 sc in next sc, sc in next sc: 76 sc.

Continued on page 7.

Rnd 5: Sc in next 36 sc, 2 sc in next sc, sc in next 4 sc, 2 sc in next sc, sc in each sc around; do **not** finish off: 78 sc.

SIDES
Rnds 1-5: Sc in each sc around.

Rnd 6: Sc in next 36 sc, place marker around last sc made for Instep placement, sc in each sc around; slip st in next sc, finish off.

INSTEP
Row 1: With **right** side facing, join Purple with slip st in marked sc on Rnd 6 of Sides; work beginning dc decrease, dc in next 6 sc, work dc decrease, sc in next sc, leave remaining sc unworked: 9 sts.

Row 2: Ch 1, turn; skip first sc, sc in next 8 dc, work sc decrease: 9 sc.

Row 3: Ch 1, turn; skip first sc, sc in next 8 sc on Instep, work sc decrease.

Rows 4 and 5: Ch 1, turn; skip first sc, sc in next 8 sc on Instep, sc in next sc on Sides.

Rows 6 and 7: Ch 1, turn; skip first sc, sc in next 8 sc on Instep, work sc decrease.

Rows 8 and 9: Ch 1, turn; skip first sc, sc in next 8 sc on Instep, sc in next sc on Sides.

Rows 10 and 11: Ch 1, turn; skip first sc, sc in next 8 sc on Instep, work sc decrease.

Row 12: Ch 1, turn; skip first sc, sc in next 8 sc on Instep, sc in next sc on Sides; finish off.

CUFF
Rnd 1: With **wrong** side facing, join White with sc in same st as joining slip st on Rnd 6 of Sides *(see Joining With Sc, page 1)*; sc in each sc across Sides to Instep, sc in first 8 sc on Row 12 of Instep, skip last sc, sc in each sc across Sides; join with slip st to first sc: 56 sc.

Rnd 2: Do **not** turn; work Loop Stitch in each sc around *(Figs. 4a-c, page 2)*: 56 Loop Sts.

Rnds 3-14: Work Loop Stitch in each Loop Stitch around.

Rnd 15: Slip st tightly in each Loop Stitch around; finish off leaving a long end for sewing.

Cut all loops and brush to resemble fur. Fold Cuff to **wrong** side and sew to Rnd 1 of Cuff.

CHILDREN'S SLIPPERS

Small	Medium	Large
7¹/₂" (19 cm)	8" (20.5 cm)	8¹/₂" (21.5 cm)

MATERIALS
Worsted Weight Yarn: **MEDIUM 4**
   White - 4{4¹/₂-4¹/₂} ounces
      225{250-250} yards
      110{130-130} grams
      205.5{228.5-228.5} meters
   Purple - 2¹/₄{2¹/₂-2¹/₂} ounces
      125{140-140} yards
      65{70-70} grams
      114.5{128-128} meters
Crochet hook as indicated below **or** size needed for gauge
   Size Small: size G (4 mm)
   Size Medium: size H (5 mm)
   Size Large: size I (5.5 mm)
Stiff bristled brush
Yarn needle

GAUGE: 16{14-12} sc and 16{14-12} rows = 4" (10 cm)

Gauge Swatch: 4" (10 cm)
With Purple, ch 17{15-13}.
Row 1: Sc in second ch from hook and in each ch across: 16{14-12} sc.
Rows 2 thru 16{14-12}: Ch 1, turn; sc in each sc across.
Finish off.

SLIPPER
SOLE
With Purple, ch 22.

Rnd 1 (Right side)**:** 2 Sc in second ch from hook, sc in next 8 chs, hdc in next 3 chs, dc in next 6 chs, 2 dc in next ch, hdc in next ch, 5 sc in last ch (toe); working in free loops of beginning ch *(Fig. 1, page 2)*, hdc in next ch, 2 dc in next ch, dc in next 6 chs, hdc in next 3 chs, sc in next 8 chs, 2 sc in same ch as first sc; do **not** join; place marker *(see Markers, page 1)*: 49 sts.

Note: Loop a short piece of yarn around any stitch to mark Rnd 1 as **right** side.

Rnd 2: 2 Sc in each of next 2 sc, sc in next 20 sts, 2 sc in next sc, (sc in next sc, 2 sc in next sc) twice, sc in next 20 sts, 2 sc in each of next 2 sc: 56 sc.

Rnd 3: Sc in next sc, 2 sc in next sc, sc in next 21 sc, 2 sc in next sc, (sc in next 2 sc, 2 sc in next sc) 3 times, sc in next 21 sc, 2 sc in next sc, sc in next sc: 62 sc.

Rnd 4: Sc in next sc, 2 sc in next sc, sc in next 24 sc, 2 sc in next sc, (sc in next 2 sc, 2 sc in next sc) 3 times, sc in next 24 sc, 2 sc in next sc, sc in next sc: 68 sc.

Rnd 5: Sc in next 32 sc, 2 sc in next sc, sc in next 4 sc, 2 sc in next sc, sc in each sc around; do **not** finish off: 70 sc.

SIDES
Rnds 1-3: Sc in each sc around.

Rnd 4: Sc in next 33 sc, place marker around last sc made for Instep placement, sc in each sc around; slip st in next sc, finish off.

INSTEP
Row 1: With **right** side facing, join Purple with slip st in marked sc on Sides, work beginning dc decrease, dc in next 4 sc, work dc decrease, sc in next sc, leave remaining sc unworked: 7 sts.

Row 2: Ch 1, turn; skip first sc, sc in next 6 dc, work sc decrease: 7 sc.

Row 3: Ch 1, turn; skip first sc, sc in next 6 sc on Instep, work sc decrease.

Rows 4 and 5: Ch 1, turn; skip first sc, sc in next 6 sc on Instep, sc in next sc on Sides.

Rows 6 and 7: Ch 1, turn; skip first sc, sc in next 6 sc on Instep, work sc decrease.

Rows 8 and 9: Ch 1, turn; skip first sc, sc in next 6 sc on Instep, sc in next sc on Sides.

Rows 10 and 11: Ch 1, turn; skip first sc, sc in next 6 sc on Instep, work sc decrease; finish off.

CUFF
Rnd 1: With **wrong** side facing, join White with sc in same st as slip st on Rnd 4 of Sides *(see Joining with Sc, page 1)*, sc in each sc across Sides to Instep, skip next sc decrease, sc in last 6 sc on Row 11 of Instep, sc in each sc across Sides: 49 sc.

Rnd 2: Do **not** turn; work Loop Stitch in each sc around *(Figs. 4a-c, page 2)*: 49 Loop Sts.

Rnds 3-12: Work Loop Stitch in each Loop Stitch around.

Rnd 13: Slip st tightly in each Loop Stitch around; finish off leaving a long end for sewing.

Cut all loops and brush to resemble fur. Fold Cuff to **wrong** side and sew to Rnd 1 of Cuff.

4. PRETTY BALLERINA

Shown on Back Cover. **EASY**
Designed by Nancy Sisk

See Size Note, page 2.

WOMEN'S SLIPPERS

Small	Medium	Large
9" (23 cm)	9¹/₂" (24 cm)	10" (25.5 cm)

MATERIALS
Worsted Weight Yarn: **MEDIUM 4**
- Dk Blue - 2¹/₂{2³/₄-2³/₄} ounces
  - 140{155-155} yards
  - 70{80-80} grams
  - 128{141.5-141.5} meters
- White - 1¹/₂ ounces, 85 yards
  - (40 grams, 77.5 meters)
- Blue - 2 yards (2 meters)
- Crochet hooks, sizes E (3.5 mm) **and** G (4 mm)
  or sizes needed for gauge
- Yarn needle

GAUGE: With larger size hook and two strands,
12 sc and 10 rows = 4" (10 cm)

Gauge Swatch: 4" (10 cm) square
With larger size hook and two strands of Dk Blue, ch 13.
Row 1: Sc in second ch from hook and in each ch across: 12 sc.
Rows 2-10: Ch 1, turn; sc in each sc across.
Finish off.

STITCH GUIDE

DECREASE
Pull up a loop in next 2 sc, YO and draw through all 3 loops on hook **(counts as one sc)**.

SLIPPER

SOLE (Make 2)
With larger size hook and two strands of Dk Blue, ch 22{25-27}.

Rnd 1 (Right side)**:** 3 Sc in second ch from hook, sc in next 9{10-11} chs, dc in next 10{12-13} chs, 5 dc in last ch (toe); working in free loops of beginning ch *(Fig. 1, page 2)*, dc in next 10{12-13} chs, sc in next 9{10-11} chs and in same ch as first sc; do **not** join, place marker *(see Markers, page 1)*: 47{53-57} sts.

Note: Loop a short piece of yarn around any stitch to mark Rnd 1 as **right** side.

Rnd 2: 2 Sc in each of next 2 sc (heel), sc in next 20{23-25} sts, 2 sc in each of next 5 dc, sc in next 20{23-25} sts: 54{60-64} sc.

Rnd 3: 2 Sc in next sc, sc in next sc, 2 sc in next sc, sc in next 21{24-26} sc, 2 sc in next sc, (sc in next sc, 2 sc in next sc) 4 times, sc in next 21{24-26} sc; do **not** finish off: 61{67-71} sc.

SIZE SMALL ONLY
Rnd 4: Sc in next 16 sc, hdc in next 11 sc, sc in next 13 sc, hdc in next 11 sc, sc in next 10 sc.

Rnd 5: Slip st in next sc, sc in next sc, 2 sc in next sc, place marker around last sc made for Sides placement, sc in next sc, slip st in next 26 sts, sc in next 5 sc, slip st in next 26 sts; finish off: 62 sts.

SIZES MEDIUM AND LARGE ONLY
Rnd 4: Sc in next {17-18} sc, dc in next {12-13} sc, sc in next 15 sc, dc in next {12-13} sc, sc in next {11-12} sc.

Rnd 5: Slip st in next 4 sc, place a marker around last slip st made for Sides placement, slip st in each st around; finish off.

9

SIDES

Rnd 1: With **wrong** sides of Soles together, working through **both** thicknesses and using smaller size hook, join one strand of White with hdc in marked st *(see Joining With Hdc, page 1)*; working in Back Loops Only *(Fig. 2, page 2)*, hdc in each st around; join with slip st to first hdc: 62{67-71} hdc.

Rnds 2 and 3: Ch 1, turn; sc in **both** loops of each st around; join with slip st to first sc.

Rnd 4: Ch 1, turn; sc in first 27{31-33} sc, decrease, (sc in next sc, decrease) 2{1-1} time(s), sc in last 27{31-33} sc; join with slip st to first sc: 59{65-69} sc.

Rnd 5: Ch 1, turn; sc in first 26{29-31} sc, decrease, sc in next 3 sc, decrease, sc in last 26{29-31} sc; join with slip st to first sc: 57{63-67} sc.

Rnd 6: Ch 1, turn; sc in first 26{29-31} sc, decrease, sc in next sc, decrease, sc in last 26{29-31} sc; join with slip st to first sc: 55{61-65} sc.

Rnd 7: Ch 1, turn; sc in first 23{31-33} sc, place marker around last sc made for Instep placement, sc in each sc around; join with slip st to first sc, finish off.

INSTEP

Row 1: With **right** side facing and using smaller size hook, join one strand of Dk Blue with sc in marked sc on Rnd 7 of Sides *(see Joining With Sc, page 1)*; sc in next 3 sc, leave remaining sc unworked: 4 sc.

Row 2: Ch 1, turn; skip first sc, sc in next 3 sc, sc in next 2 sc on Sides: 5 sc.

Row 3: Ch 1, turn; skip first sc, sc in next 4 sc on Instep, sc in next 2 sc on Sides: 6 sc.

Rows 4-7: Ch 1, turn; skip first sc, sc in each sc across Instep, sc in next 2 sc on Sides: 10 sc.

SIZE SMALL ONLY

Row 8: Ch 1, turn; sc in each sc across; finish off.

SIZES MEDIUM AND LARGE ONLY

Row 8: Ch 1, turn; skip first sc, sc in each sc on Instep, sc in next 2 sc on Sides: 11 sc.

Row 9: Ch 1, turn; sc in each sc across; finish off.

EDGING

With **right** side facing and using smaller size hook, join one strand of Dk Blue with sc in same st as joining on Rnd 7 of Sides; sc in each sc around; join with slip st to first sc; finish off.

Using photo as a guide for placement, embroider Flower onto center of Instep as follows: Using one strand of Blue and Lazy Daisy Stitch *(Fig. 6)*, make 8 petals. With Dk Blue, work French knot *(Fig. 7)* in center of Flower.

Fig. 6

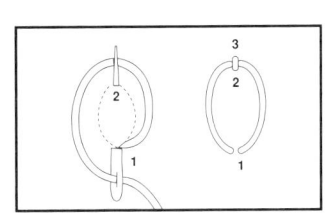

Fig. 7

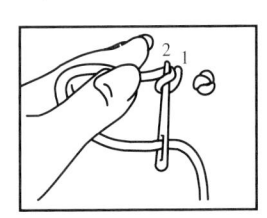

CHILDREN'S SLIPPERS

Small	Medium	Large
7 1/2" (19 cm)	8" (20.5 cm)	8 1/2" (21.5 cm)

MATERIALS

Worsted Weight Yarn: **MEDIUM 4**
  Dk Blue - 2 1/4{2 1/4-2 1/2} ounces
    125{125-140} yards
    65{65-70} grams
    114.5{114.5-128} meters
  White - 1 1/4 ounces, 70 yards
    (35 grams, 65 meters)
  Blue - 2 yards (2 meters)
Crochet hooks, sizes E (3.5 mm) **and** G (4 mm)
  or sizes needed for gauge
Yarn needle

GAUGE: With larger size hook and two strands,
  12 sc and 10 rows = 4" (10 cm)

Gauge Swatch: 4" (10 cm) square
With larger size hook and two strands of Dk Blue, ch 13.
Row 1: Sc in second ch from hook and in each ch across.
Rows 2-10: Ch 1, turn; sc in each sc across.
Finish off.

Continued on page 11.

SLIPPER
SOLE
With larger size hook and two strands of Dk Blue, ch 18{20-22}.

Rnd 1 (Right side): 3 Sc in second ch from hook, sc in next 7{8-9} chs, dc in next 8{9-10} chs, 5 dc in last ch (toe); working in free loops of beginning ch *(Fig. 1, page 2)*, dc in next 8{9-10} chs, sc in next 7{8-9} chs and in same ch as first sc; do **not** join, place marker *(see Markers, page 1)*: 39{43-47} sts.

Note: Loop a short piece of yarn around any stitch to mark Rnd 1 as **right** side.

Rnd 2: 2 Sc in each of next 2 sc (heel), sc in next 16{18-20} sts, 2 sc in each of next 5 dc, sc in next 16{18-20} sts: 46{50-54} sc.

Rnd 3: 2 Sc in next sc, sc in next sc, 2 sc in next sc, sc in next 17{19-21} sc, 2 sc in next sc, (sc in next sc, 2 sc in next sc) 4 times, sc in next 17{19-21} sc: 53{57-61} sc.

SIZE SMALL ONLY
Rnd 4: Sc in next 3 sc, place marker around last sc made for Sides placement, sc in each sc around; slip st in next sc, finish off.

SIZES MEDIUM AND LARGE ONLY
Rnd 4: Sc in next 3 sc, place marker around last sc made for Sides placement, sc in next {12-13} sc, dc in next {10-11} sc, sc in next 13 sc, dc in next {10-11} sc, sc in next {9-10} sc; slip st in next sc, finish off.

SIDES
Rnd 1: With **right** side facing and using smaller size hook, join one strand of White with hdc in marked sc *(see Joining With Hdc, page 1)*; working in Back Loops Only *(Fig. 2, page 2)*, hdc in each st around; join with slip st to first hdc: 53{57-61} hdc.

Rnds 2-4: Ch 1, turn; sc in **both** loops of each st around; join with slip st to first sc.

Rnd 5: Ch 1, turn; sc in first 24{26-28} sc, decrease, sc in next sc, decrease, sc in last 24{26-28} sc; join with slip st to first sc: 51{55-59} sc.

Rnd 6: Ch 1, turn; sc in first 22{24-26} sc, decrease, sc in next 3 sc, decrease, sc in last 22{24-26} sc; join with slip st to first sc: 49{53-57} sc.

Rnd 7: Ch 1, turn; sc in first 22{24-26} sc, decrease, sc in next sc, decrease, sc in last 22{24-26} sc; join with slip st to first sc: 47{51-55} sc.

Rnd 8: Ch 1, turn; sc in first 25{27-29} sc, place marker around last sc made for Instep placement, sc in each sc around; join with slip st to first sc, finish off.

INSTEP
Row 1: With **right** side facing and using smaller size hook, join one strand of Dk Blue with sc in marked sc on Rnd 8 of Sides *(see Joining With Sc, page 1)*; sc in next 3 sc: 4 sc.

Row 2: Ch 1, turn; skip first sc, sc in next 3 sc, sc in next 2 sc on Sides: 5 sc.

Row 3: Ch 1, turn; skip first sc, sc in next 4 sc on Instep, sc in next 2 sc on Sides: 6 sc.

Rows 4-7: Ch 1, turn; skip first sc, sc in each sc across Instep, sc in next 2 sc on Sides: 10 sc.

SIZE SMALL ONLY
Row 8: Ch 1, turn; sc in each sc across; finish off.

SIZES MEDIUM AND LARGE ONLY
Row 8: Ch 1, turn; skip first sc, sc in each sc on Instep, sc in next 2 sc on Sides: 11 sc.

Row 9: Ch 1, turn; sc in each sc across; finish off.

EDGING
With **right** side facing and using smaller size hook, join one strand of Dk Blue with sc in same st as joining on Rnd 8 of Sides; sc in each sc around; join with slip st to first sc, finish off.

Using photo as a guide for placement, embroider Flower onto center of Instep as follows: Using one strand of Blue and Lazy Daisy Stitch *(Fig. 6, page 10)*, make 8 petals. With Dk Blue, work French knot *(Fig. 7, page 10)* in center of Flower.

5. COMFY SANDALS

Shown on Back Cover. ◼◼◻◻ **EASY**
Designed by Marian Brodman

See Size Note, page 2.

WOMEN'S SLIPPERS

Small	Medium	Large
9" (23 cm)	9½" (24 cm)	10" (25.5 cm)

MATERIALS
Worsted Weight Yarn: **MEDIUM 4**
- 4¾{5-5¼} ounces
- 260{270-285} yards
- 135{140-150} grams
- 237.5{247-260.5} meters

Crochet hook, size G (4 mm) **or** size needed for gauge
Plastic canvas - 10½" x 13½" piece (26.5 cm x 34.5 cm)
Yarn needle

GAUGE: 12 sc and 10 rows = 4" (10 cm)

Gauge Swatch: 4" (10 cm) square
With two strands of yarn, ch 13.
Row 1: Sc in second ch from hook and in each ch across.
Rows 2-10: Ch 1, turn; sc in each sc across.

Note: Sandals are worked holding two strands of yarn together throughout.

SANDAL

SOLE (Make 2)
Ch 22{25-27}.

Rnd 1 (Right side): 3 Sc in second ch from hook, sc in next 9{10-11} chs, dc in next 10{12-13} chs, 5 dc in last ch (toe); working in free loops of beginning ch *(Fig. 1, page 2)*, dc in next 10{12-13} chs, sc in next 9{10-11} chs and in same ch as first sc; do **not** join, place marker *(see Markers, page 1)*: 47{53-57} sts.

Note: Loop a short piece of yarn around any stitch to mark Rnd 1 as **right** side.

Rnd 2: 2 Sc in each of next 2 sc (heel), sc in next 20{23-25} sts, 2 sc in each of next 5 dc, sc in next 20{23-25} sts: 54{60-64} sc.

Rnd 3: 2 Sc in next sc, sc in next sc, 2 sc in next sc, sc in next 21{24-26} sc, 2 sc in next sc, (sc in next sc, 2 sc in next sc) 4 times, sc in next 21{24-26} sc; do **not** finish off: 61{67-71} sc.

SIZE SMALL ONLY
Rnd 4: Sc in next 16 sc, hdc in next 11 sc, sc in next 13 sc, hdc in next 11 sc, sc in next 10 sc.

Rnd 5: Slip st in next sc, sc in next sc, 2 sc in next sc, sc in next sc, slip st in next 26 sts, sc in next 5 sc, slip st in next 26 sts; finish off: 62 sts.

SIZES MEDIUM AND LARGE ONLY
Rnd 4: Sc in next {17-18} sc, dc in next {12-13} sc, sc in next 15 sc, dc in next {12-13} sc, sc in next {11-12} sc.

Rnd 5: Slip st in each st around; finish off.

STRAP (Make 2)
Ch 17{18-19}.

Row 1: Sc in second ch from hook and in each ch across: 16{17-18} sc.

Row 2 (Right side): Ch 1, turn; sc in each sc across.

Note: Loop a short piece of yarn around any stitch to mark Row 2 as **right** side.

Rows 3 and 4: Ch 1, turn; sc in each sc across.

Finish off.

Continued on page 13.

ASSEMBLY

Using Sole as a pattern, cut one piece of plastic canvas ¹/₄" (7 mm) smaller than Sole. Insert piece of plastic canvas between Soles with **wrong** sides together. Matching sts and working through **inside** loops only, whipstitch Soles together *(Fig. 5b, page 2)*.

Using photo as guide, cross 2 Straps and sew to each edge of Sole, placing Straps to hold foot securely.

CHILDREN'S SLIPPERS

Small	Medium	Large
7¹/₂" (19 cm)	8" (20.5 cm)	8¹/₂" (21.5 cm)

MATERIALS
Worsted Weight Yarn: **MEDIUM 4**
  4{4¹/₄-4¹/₂} ounces
  220{230-250} yards
  110{120-130} grams
  201{210.5-228.5} meters
Crochet hook, size G (4 mm) **or** size needed for gauge
Plastic canvas - 10¹/₂" x 13¹/₂" piece
  (26.5 cm x 34.5 cm)
Yarn needle

GAUGE: 12 sc and 10 rows = 4" (10 cm)

Gauge Swatch: 4" (10 cm) square
With two strands of yarn, ch 13.
Row 1: Sc in second ch from hook and in each ch across: 12 sc.
Rows 2-10: Ch 1, turn; sc in each sc across.

Note: Sandals are worked holding two strands of yarn together throughout.

SANDAL
SOLE (Make 2)
Ch 18{20-22}.

Rnd 1 (Right side): 3 Sc in second ch from hook, sc in next 7{8-9} chs, dc in next 8{9-10} chs, 5 dc in last ch (toe); working in free loops of beginning ch *(Fig. 1, page 2)*, dc in next 8{9-10} chs, sc in next 8{9-10} chs; do **not** join, place marker *(see Markers, page 1)*: 39{43-47} sts.

Note: Loop a short piece of yarn around any stitch to mark Rnd 1 as **right** side.

Rnd 2: 2 Sc in each of next 2 sc, sc in next 16{18-20} sts, 2 sc in each of next 5 dc, sc in next 16{18-20} sts: 46{50-54} sc.

Rnd 3: 2 Sc in next sc, sc in next sc, 2 sc in next sc, sc in next 17{19-21} sc, 2 sc in next sc, (sc in next sc, 2 sc in next sc) 4 times, sc in next 17{19-21} sc; do **not** finish off: 53{57-61} sc.

SIZE SMALL ONLY
Rnd 4: Sc in each sc around; do **not** finish off.

SIZES MEDIUM AND LARGE ONLY
Rnd 4: Sc in next {15-16} sc, hdc in next {10-11} sc, sc in next 13 sc, hdc in next {10-11} sc, sc in next {9-10} sc, do **not** finish off.

ALL SIZES
Rnd 5: Slip st in each st around; finish off.

STRAP (Make 2)
Ch 15{16-17}.

Row 1: Sc in second ch from hook and in each ch across: 14{15-16} sc.

Row 2 (Right side): Ch 1, turn; sc in each sc across.

Note: Loop a short piece of yarn around any stitch to mark Row 2 as **right** side.

Row 3: Ch 1, turn; sc in each sc across; finish off.

ASSEMBLY

Using Sole as a pattern, cut one piece of plastic canvas ¹/₄" (7 mm) smaller than Sole. Insert piece of plastic canvas between Soles with **wrong** sides together. Matching sts and working through **inside** loops only, whipstitch Soles together *(Fig. 5b, page 2)*.

Using photo as guide, cross 2 Straps and sew to each edge of Sole, placing Straps to hold foot securely.

6. TOOTSIE WARMERS

Shown on Front Cover. **EASY**
Designed by Joyce Shelton

See Size Note, page 2.

WOMEN'S SLIPPERS

Small	Medium	Large
9" (23 cm)	9 1/2" (24 cm)	10" (25.5 cm)

MATERIALS
Worsted Weight Yarn: **MEDIUM 4**
- 5 1/4{5 1/2-5 3/4} ounces
- 340{360-375} yards
- 150{160-165} grams
- 311{329-343} meters

Crochet hook, size G (4 mm) **or** size needed for gauge
Yarn needle

GAUGE: 12 sc and 12 rows = 4" (10 cm)

Gauge Swatch: 4" (10 cm) square
With two strands of yarn, ch 13.
Row 1: Sc in second ch from hook and in each ch across: 12 sc.
Rows 2-12: Ch 1, turn; sc in each sc across.

STITCH GUIDE

DECREASE
Pull up a loop in next 2 sc, YO and draw through all 3 loops on hook (**counts as one sc**).

Note: Slippers are made holding two strands of yarn together throughout.

SLIPPER
SOLE
Ch 7{7-8}.

Row 1 (Wrong side)**:** Sc in second ch from hook and in each ch across: 6{6-7} sc.

Note: Loop a short piece of yarn around **back** of any stitch to mark **right** side.

Rows 2-5: Ch 1, turn; 2 sc in first sc, sc in each sc across: 10{10-11} sc.

Rows 6 thru 7{9-11}: Ch 1, turn; sc in each sc across.

Rows 8{10-12} thru 10{12-14}: Ch 1, turn; decrease, sc in each sc across: 7{7-8} sc.

Row 11{13-15}: Ch 1, turn; sc in each sc across.

Repeat Row 11{13-15} until Sole measures 8 1/2{9-9 1/2}"/21.5{23-24} cm from beginning ch, ending by working a **right** side row.

Next Row: Ch 1, turn; decrease, sc in next 3{3-4} sc, decrease: 5{5-6} sc.

Last Row: Ch 1, turn; decrease, sc in next 1{1-2} sc, decrease; finish off: 3{3-4} sc.

INSTEP
Ch 8{8-9}.

Row 1: Sc in second ch from hook and in each ch across: 7{7-8} sc.

Row 2: Ch 1, turn; working in Back Loops Only (*Fig. 2, page 2*), 2 sc in first sc, sc in each sc across: 8{8-9} sc.

Rows 3 thru 13{15-16}: Repeat Row 2, 11{13-14} times: 19{21-23} sc.

Rows 14{16-17} and 15{17-18}: Ch 1, turn; sc in Back Loop Only of each sc across; do **not** finish off.

Continued on page 15.

SIDES
FIRST SIDE
Row 1 (Right side)**:** Sc in Back Loop Only of first 7{8-9} sc, leave remaining 12{13-14} sc unworked.

Note: Loop a short piece of yarn around any stitch to mark Row 1 as **right** side.

Row 2: Ch 1, turn; sc in Back Loop Only of each sc across.

Repeat Row 2 until First Side is long enough to reach center back of Sole; finish off.

SECOND SIDE
Row 1: With **right** side facing and working in Back Loops Only, skip next 5 sc from First Side and join yarn with sc in next sc *(see Joining With Sc, page 1)*; sc in each sc across: 7{8-9} sc.

Row 2: Ch 1, turn; sc in Back Loop Only of each sc across.

Repeat Row 2 until Second Side measures same as First Side; finish off.

ASSEMBLY
Sew back seam of Sides together. With **wrong** sides of Sole and Instep together and working through **both** thicknesses, join yarn with sc in center sc on toe of **both** piece; sc around matching back seam to center sc on Sole heel; join with slip st to first sc, finish off.

CHILDREN'S SLIPPERS

Small	Medium	Large
7½" (19 cm)	8" (20.5 cm)	8½" (21.5 cm)

MATERIALS
Worsted Weight Yarn: **MEDIUM 4**
  4½{4¾-5} ounces
  295{310-325} yards
  130{135-140} grams
  269.5{283.5-297} meters
Crochet hook, size G (4 mm) **or** size needed for gauge
Yarn needle

GAUGE: 12 sc and 12 rows = 4" (10 cm)

Gauge Swatch: 4" (10 cm) square
With two strands of yarn, ch 13.
Row 1: Sc in second ch from hook and in each ch across: 12 sc.
Rows 2-12: Ch 1, turn; sc in each sc across.

Note: Slippers are made holding two strands of yarn throughout.

SLIPPER
SOLES
Ch 6{6-7}.

Row 1 (Wrong side)**:** Sc in second ch from hook and in each ch across: 5{5-6} sc.

Note: Loop a short piece of yarn around **back** of any stitch to mark **right** side.

Rows 2-5: Ch 1, turn; 2 sc in first sc, sc in each sc across: 9{9-10} sc.

Rows 6 thru 11{12-13}: Ch 1, turn; sc in each sc across.

Rows 12{13-14} and 13{14-15}: Ch 1, turn; decrease, sc in each sc across: 7{7-8} sc.

Row 14{15-16}: Ch 1, turn; sc in each sc across.

Repeat Row 14{15-16} until Sole measures 7{7^{1}/$_{2}$-8}"/18{19-20.5} cm from beginning ch, ending by working a **right** side row.

Next Row: Ch 1, turn; decrease, sc in next 3{3-4} sc, decrease: 5{5-6} sc.

Last Row: Ch 1, turn; decrease, sc in next 1{1-2} sc, decrease; finish off: 3{3-4} sc.

INSTEP
Ch 7{7-8}.

Row 1: Sc in second ch from hook and in each ch across: 6{6-7} sc.

Row 2: Ch 1, turn; working in Back Loops Only *(Fig. 2, page 2)*, 2 sc in first sc, sc in each sc across: 7{7-8} sc.

Rows 3 thru 12{12-13}: Repeat Row 2, 10{10-11} times: 17{17-19} sc.

Rows 13{13-14} and 14{14-15}: Ch 1, turn; sc in each sc across; do **not** finish off.

SIDES
FIRST SIDE
Row 1 (Right side)**:** Sc in Back Loop Only of first 6{6-7} sc, leave remaining 11{11-12} sc unworked.

Note: Loop a short piece of yarn around any stitch to mark Row 1 as **right** side.

Row 2: Ch 1, turn; sc in Back Loop Only of each sc across.

Repeat Row 2 until First Side is long enough to reach center back of Sole; finish off.

SECOND SIDE
Row 1: With **right** side facing and working in Back Loops Only, skip next 5 sc from First Side and join yarn with sc in next sc *(see Joining With Sc, page 1)*; sc in each sc across: 6{6-7} sc.

Row 2: Ch 1, turn; sc in Back Loop Only of each sc across.

Repeat Row 2 until Second Side measures same as First Side; finish off.

ASSEMBLY
Sew back seam of Sides together. With **wrong** sides of Sole and Instep together, working through **both** thicknesses, join yarn with sc in center sc on toe of **both** pieces, sc around matching back seam to center sc on Sole heel; finish off.

7. PRETTY IN PINK

Shown on Front Cover. **EASY**
Designed by Mary A. Watkins

See Size Note, page 2.

WOMEN'S SLIPPERS

Small
9" (23 cm)

Medium
9 1/2" (24 cm)

Large
10" (25.5 cm)

MATERIALS
Worsted Weight Yarn: **MEDIUM 4**
  3 3/4{4-4 1/4} ounces
  245{260-275} yards
  105{110-120} grams
  224{237.5-251.5} meters
Crochet hook, size H (5 mm) **or** size needed for gauge
Yarn needle

GAUGE: 16 hdc and 8 rows = 4" (10 cm)

Gauge Swatch: 4" (10 cm) square
Ch 17.
Row 1: Hdc in third ch from hook **(2 skipped chs count as first hdc)** and in each ch across: 16 hdc.
Rows 2-8: Ch 2 **(counts as first hdc)**, turn; hdc in next hdc and in each hdc across.
Finish off.

BODY
Ch 37{39-41}.

Row 1: Hdc in third ch from hook **(2 skipped chs count as first hdc)** and in each ch across: 36{38-40} hdc.

Rows 2-18: Ch 2 **(counts as first hdc, now and throughout)**, turn; working in Back Loops Only *(Fig. 2, page 2)*, hdc in next hdc and in each hdc across.

Joining Row (Instep): Ch 1, turn; fold lengthwise having beginning ch behind Row 18, working in Back Loops Only of Row 18 and in free loops of beginning ch *(Fig. 1, page 2)*, sc in first 15 sts, leave remaining sts unworked to form opening; finish off.

Thread yarn needle with an 18" (45.5 cm) length and weave through end of rows at toe; gather tightly and secure ends.

Sew heel seam, matching rows.

FLOWER
Ch 24.

Row 1: Dc in fourth ch from hook, ★ ch 2, skip next ch, dc in next ch; repeat from ★ across: 11 dc and 10 ch-2 sps.

Row 2 (Right side): Ch 1, turn; 5 dc in first ch-2 sp **(petal made)**, sc in next dc, ★ 5 dc in next ch-2 sp, sc in next dc; repeat from ★ 8 times **more**, 5 dc in ch-3 on end of Row 1, sc in free loop of next ch (ch at base of first dc on Row 1); finish off leaving a long end for sewing: 11 petals.

Note: Loop a short piece of yarn around any stitch to mark Row 2 as **right** side.

With **right** side facing, beginning with last petal in center of Flower, **loosely** wrap remaining petals around.
Using long end, sew Flower securely to Instep of Slipper.

CHILDREN'S SLIPPERS

Small	Medium	Large
7$\frac{1}{2}$" (19 cm)	8" (20.5 cm)	8$\frac{1}{2}$" (21.5 cm)

MATERIALS
Worsted Weight Yarn: **MEDIUM 4**
 3$\frac{1}{4}${3$\frac{1}{2}$-3$\frac{1}{2}$} ounces
 210{230-230} yards
 95{100-100} grams
 192{210.5-210.5} meters
Crochet hook, size H (5 mm) **or** size needed for gauge
Yarn needle

GAUGE: 16 hdc and 8 rows = 4" (10 cm)

Gauge Swatch: 4" (10 cm) square
Ch 17.
Row 1: Hdc in third ch from hook **(2 skipped chs count as first hdc)** and in each ch across: 16 hdc.
Rows 2-8: Ch 2 **(counts as first hdc)**, turn; hdc in next hdc and in each hdc across.
Finish off.

BODY
Ch 31{33-35}.

Row 1: Hdc in third ch from hook **(2 skipped chs count as first hdc)** and in each ch across: 30{32-34} hdc.

Rows 2-18: Ch 2 **(counts as first hdc, now and throughout)**, turn; working in Back Loops Only *(Fig. 2, page 2)*, hdc in next hdc and in each hdc across.

Joining Row (Instep): Ch 1, turn; fold lengthwise having beginning ch behind Row 18, working in Back Loops Only of Row 18 and in free loops of beginning ch *(Fig. 1, page 2)*, sc in first 15 sts, leave remaining sts unworked to form opening; finish off.

Thread yarn needle with an 18" (45.5 cm) length and weave through end of rows at toe; gather tightly and secure ends.

Sew heel seam, matching rows.

FLOWER
Ch 24.

Row 1: Dc in fourth ch from hook, ★ ch 2, skip next ch, dc in next ch; repeat from ★ across: 11 dc and 10 ch-2 sps.

Row 2 (Right side): Ch 1, turn; 5 dc in first ch-2 sp **(petal made)**, sc in next dc, ★ 5 dc in next ch-2 sp, sc in next dc; repeat from ★ 8 times **more**, 5 dc in ch-3 on end of Row 1, sc in free loop of next ch (ch at base of first dc on Row 1); finish off leaving a long end for sewing: 11 petals.

Note: Loop a short piece of yarn around any stitch to mark Row 2 as **right** side.

With **right** side facing, beginning with last petal in center of Flower, **loosely** wrap remaining petals around.
Using long end, sew Flower securely to Instep of Slipper.

8. TOASTY SLIP-ONS

Shown on Back Cover. ■■□□ EASY
Designed by Barbara Earls

See Size Note, page 2.

WOMEN'S SLIPPERS

Small	Medium	Large
9" (23 cm)	9½" (24 cm)	10" (25.5 cm)

MATERIALS
Worsted Weight Yarn: 🏷️ 4 MEDIUM
 Brown - 4{4½-4½} ounces
  225{250-250} yards
  110{130-130} grams
  205.5{228.5-228.5} meters
 Dk Brown - 28 yards (25.5 meters)
Crochet hook as indicated below **or** size needed for gauge
 Size Small: size G (4 mm)
 Size Medium: size H (5 mm)
 Size Large: size I (5.5 mm)
Yarn needle

GAUGE: 14{12-10} hdc
 and 12{10-8} rnds = 4" (10 cm)

Gauge Swatch: 4" (10 cm) square
With Brown, ch 15{13-11}.
Row 1: Hdc in second ch from hook and in each ch across: 14{12-10} hdc.
Rows 2 thru 12{10-8}: Ch 1, turn; hdc in each hdc across.
Finish off.

STITCH GUIDE

DECREASE
Pull up a loop in next 2 sts, YO and draw through all 3 loops on hook **(counts as one sc)**.

TREBLE CROCHET *(abbreviated tr)*
YO twice, insert hook in st indicated, YO and pull up a loop (4 loops on hook), (YO and draw through 2 loops on hook) 3 times.

SLIPPER
SOLE
With Brown, ch 20.

Rnd 1 (Right side): Sc in second ch from hook and in next 17 chs, 5 sc in last ch (toe), working in free loops of beginning ch *(Fig. 1, page 2)*, sc in next 17 chs, 4 sc in same ch as first sc (heel); do **not** join, place marker *(see Markers, page 1)*: 44 sc.

Note: Loop a short piece of yarn around any stitch to mark Rnd 1 as **right** side.

Rnd 2: Hdc in next 20 sc, 3 hdc in next sc, hdc in next 21 sc, 3 hdc in next sc, hdc in next sc: 48 hdc.

Rnd 3: Hdc in next 22 hdc, 5 hdc in next hdc, hdc in next 23 hdc, 5 hdc in next hdc, hdc in next hdc: 56 hdc.

Rnd 4: Hdc in next 24 hdc, 3 hdc in next hdc, hdc in next 27 hdc, 3 hdc in next hdc, hdc in next 3 hdc: 60 hdc.

Rnd 5: Hdc in next 26 hdc, 5 hdc in next hdc, hdc in next 29 hdc, 5 hdc in next hdc, hdc in next 3 hdc: 68 hdc.

Rnd 6: Hdc in next 9 hdc, decrease, sc in next 17 hdc, 3 sc in next hdc, sc in next 17 hdc, decrease, hdc in next 14 hdc, 3 hdc in next hdc, hdc in next 5 hdc; do **not** finish off: 70 sts.

SIDES

Rnd 1: Working in Back Loops Only *(Fig. 2, page 2)*, sc in next 9 hdc, decrease, sc in next 35 sc, decrease, sc in next 22 hdc: 68 sc.

Rnd 2: Working in **both** loops, hdc in next 14 sc, sc in next 29 sc, hdc in next 25 sc.

Rnd 3: Hdc in next 14 hdc, sc in next 29 sc, hdc in next 25 hdc.

Rnd 4: Hdc in next 14 hdc, 2 sc in next sc, sc in next 27 sc, 2 sc in next sc, hdc in next 25 hdc: 70 sts.

Rnd 5: Hdc in next 14 hdc, 2 sc in next sc, sc in next 29 sc, 2 sc in next sc, hdc in next 25 hdc: 72 sts.

Rnd 6: Hdc in next 14 hdc, sc in next 33 sc, hdc in next 25 hdc.

Rnd 7: Hdc in next 15 sts, sc in next 33 sts, hdc in next 24 sts; slip st in next hdc, finish off.

CUFF

With **right** side facing and working in Front Loops Only, join Brown with slip st in first hdc on Row 7 of Sides; ch 4 **(counts as first tr, now and throughout)**, tr in next 38 sts, leave remaining 33 sc unworked; finish off: 39 tr.

With **right** side facing, using one strand of Dk Brown and matching sts on Rnd 5 of Sides, fold Cuff to **right** side and sew to Rnd 5 of Sides, forming a casing.

INSTEP

With Brown, ch 9.

Row 1 (Right side): Sc in second ch from hook and in each ch across: 8 sc.

Note: Loop a short piece of yarn around any stitch to mark Row 1 as **right** side.

Work in Back Loops Only throughout.

Rows 2-10: Ch 1, turn; sc in each sc across.

Row 11: Ch 1, turn; sc in first 6 sc, decrease: 7 sc.

Row 12: Ch 1, turn; sc in first 5 sc, decrease: 6 sc.

Row 13: Ch 1, turn; sc in each sc across.

Row 14: Ch 1, turn; sc in first 4 sc, decrease: 5 sc.

Row 15: Ch 1, turn; sc in first 3 sc, decrease: 4 sc.

Row 16: Ch 1, turn; sc in first 2 sc, decrease; finish off: 3 sc.

Tab: With **right** side facing, and working in free loops of beginning ch *(Fig. 1, page 2)*, join Brown with slip st in first ch; ch 4, tr in next ch, 2 tr in next ch, tr in next 2 chs, 2 tr in next ch, tr in last 2 chs; finish off: 10 tr.

With **right** side facing, using two strands of Dk Brown and matching end of rows to sc on Rnd 7 of Sides, sew Instep to Sides, leaving Tab unsewn.

TIE

With two strands of Dk Brown, ch a 36" length; finish off.
Tie a knot at both ends of Tie.

Finishing: With **right** side facing, weave Tie through casing.

With toe facing you, weave first end of Tie behind first tr on Tab, weave in front of next 2 tr, weave behind next tr.

With toe facing you, weave second end of Tie behind last tr on Tab, weave in front of next 2 tr, weave behind next tr.

Tie ends in a bow.

YARN INFORMATION

Each Slipper in this leaflet was made with Worsted Weight Yarn. Any brand of Worsted Weight Yarn may be used. It is best to refer to the yardage/meters when determining how many balls or skeins to purchase. Remember, to arrive at the finished size, it is the GAUGE/TENSION that is important, not the brand of yarn.

For your convenience, the specific yarns used to create our photography models, are listed in the next column.

We have made every effort to ensure that these instructions are accurate and complete. We cannot, however, be responsible for human error, typographical mistakes, or variations in individual work.

Production Team:
Instructional Editor - Lisa Rickman
Technical Editor - Lois J. Long
Lead Graphic Artist - Rachel Brugess
Graphic Artist - Rebecca J. Hester
Photo Stylist - Cassie Newsome
Photographer - Russ Ganser

Slippers made and instructions tested by Janet Akins, Marianna Crowder, and Kay Meadors.

1. FUZZY WUZZIES
Bernat® So Soft®
#9875 Scarlet

2. LILAC SQUARES
Bernat® Berella® "4"®
Dk Green - #1235 Soft Green
Green - #1232 Gentle Green
Purple - #8712 Lilac Petal

3. PURPLE PASSION
Bernat® Berella® "4"®
White - #8941 Winter White
Purple - #8724 Velvet Night

4. PRETTY BALLERINA
Bernat® Berella® "4"®
Dk Blue - #1141 Rich Periwinkle Blue
White - #8941 Winter White
Blue - #1143 Soft Periwinkle Blue

5. COMFY SANDALS
Red Heart ®TLC® Essentials™
#2335 Taupe

6. TOOTSIE WARMERS
Patons® Canadiana
#032 Bright Royal Blue

7. PRETTY IN PINK
Patons® Canadiana
#10728 Hot Fuchsia

8. TOASTY SLIP-ONS
Bernat® Berella® "4"®
Brown - #1011 Soft Taupe
Dk Brown - #1012 True Taupe